Tea with Oliver

by Mika Song

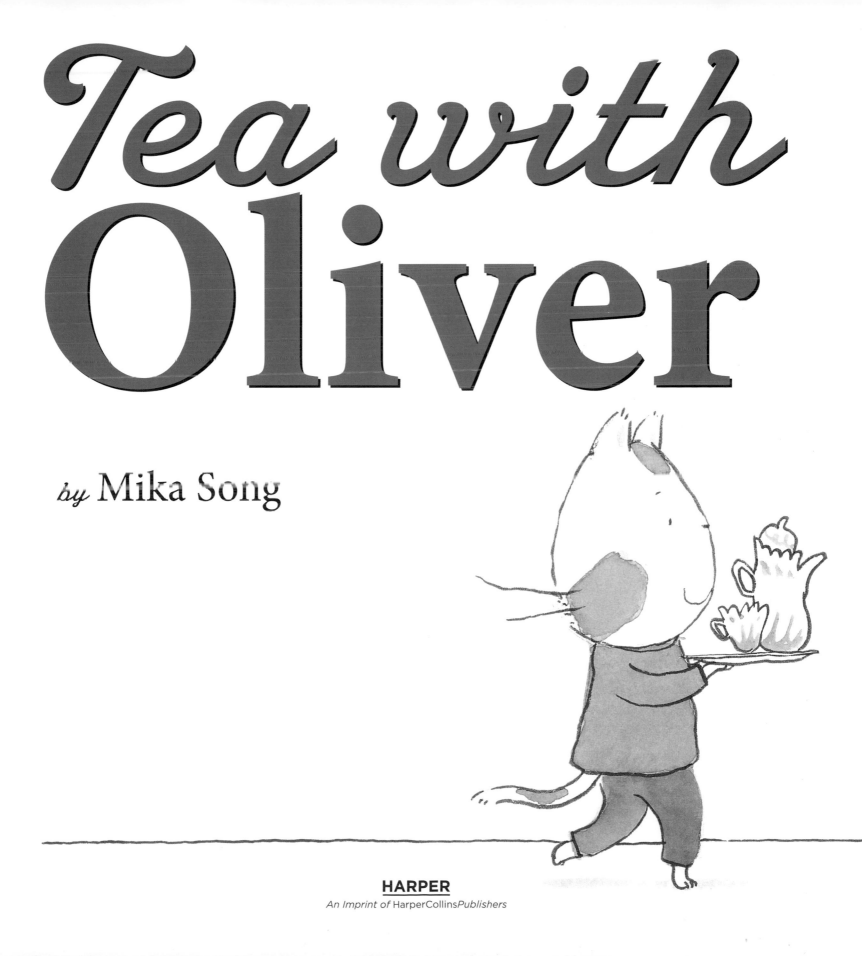

HARPER
An Imprint of HarperCollinsPublishers

To Jae

Tea with Oliver
Copyright © 2017 by Mika Song
All rights reserved. Manufactured in China.
No part of this book may be used or reproduced in any manner whatsoever without written permission except
in the case of brief quotations embodied in critical articles and reviews. For information address
HarperCollins Children's Books, a division of HarperCollins Publishers, 195 Broadway, New York, NY 10007.

www.harpercollinschildrens.com

ISBN 978-0-06-242948-3 (trade bdg.)

The artist used ink and watercolor to create the illustrations for this book.

Typography by Mika Song and Chelsea C. Donaldson

17 18 19 20 21   SCP   10 9 8 7 6 5 4 3 2 1
❖
First Edition

Oliver talks to himself a lot.

Philbert talks to Oliver a lot.
But Philbert is too shy to come
out from under the couch.

And Oliver doesn't hear him.

So Philbert decides to write Oliver a letter.

But whoops! Oliver sweeps the note back under the couch.

So Philbert tries again. This time he sends his letter by airmail . . .

but Oliver thinks it's a bug,

and he misses the letter again.

Philbert wonders what to do. Then there's a knock on the door.

So Philbert decides to march right up and hand Oliver the letter.

But just then the guests arrive and the party begins.

Oliver is excited—someone at the party *must* want tea.

Tea?

No, we're dancing, silly!

Me! I want tea.

The party ends as quickly as it began.

Oliver rolls over and finds . . . a mouse!

Philbert hands him the letter.

And the new friends sit down for a nice cup of tea.

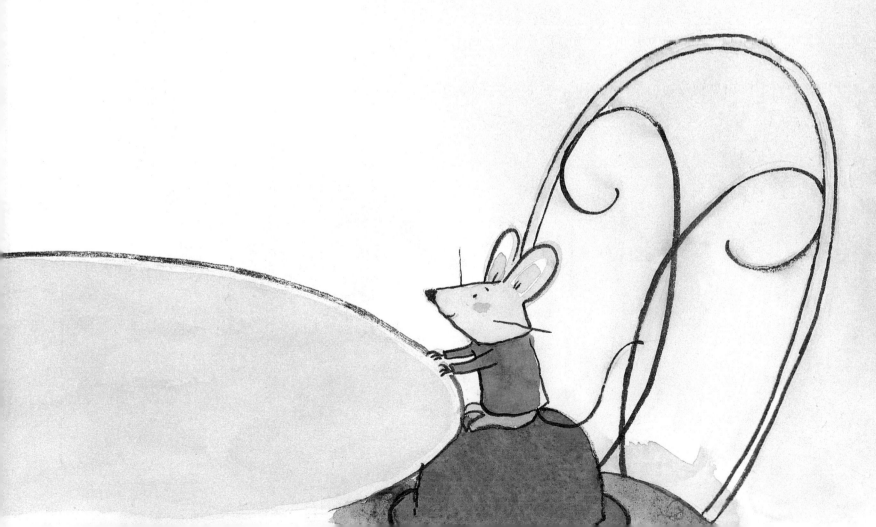

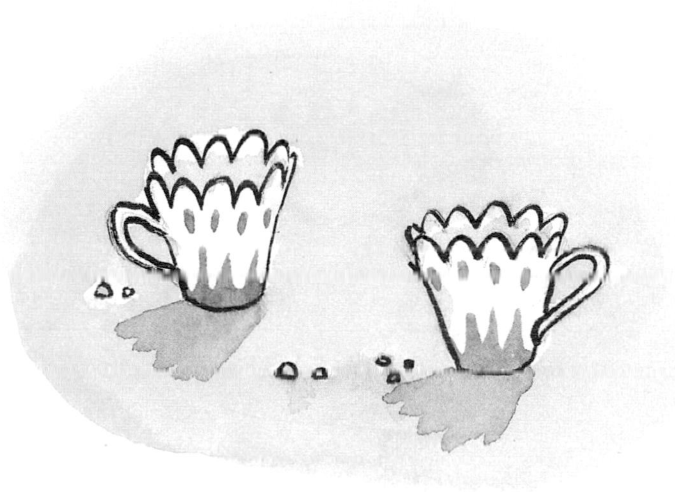

Dear Oliver,
I am your
neighbor.
Your pal,
Philbert

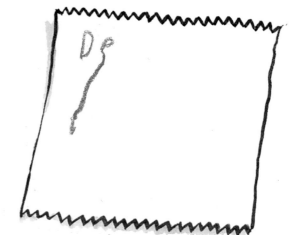
D
!

Dear Oliver,
cookies go well
with tea. Any
type of cookie.
P.

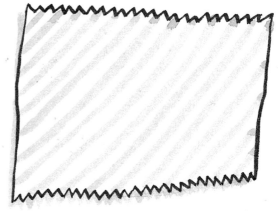

Dear Oliver,
Tea is best
with a friend.
Your true friend,
Philbert

Hi!
From under
the couch,
P.